Too Late For Manly Hands

Too Late for Manly Hands

Poems

Hank Jones

Acknowledgments

Several poems included here appeared in the following publications:

"Close Kin"
    Cybersoleil: A Literary Journal (2014)

"If You Put the Words Together Just Right"
    Dragon Poet Review (Winter 2014)

"Michael and I Buy Cigars on Bourbon Street"
    Dragon Poet Review (Summer 2015)

"Too Late for Manly Hands"
    Concho River Review (Spring 2016)

"What I Learned in Boy Scouts" and "Mosquito"
    The Great American Wise Ass Anthology (Lamar University Literary Press 2016)

"More Books to Read, More Life to Lead" and "First Rifle"
    Voices de la Luna (15 February 2016, Volume 8, Issue 2)

"Stone Shrine"
    Stone Renga (Tale Feathers Press 2017)

"A View of Life Through the Lens of Cancer" and
"Waiting on the PET Scan"
    Red River Review (November 2017)

"Somewhere between Belief and Disbelief"
    Speak Your Mind: Poems of Protest & Resistance (Village Books Press 2019)

"Potroast and Poetry"
    Bull Buffalo & Indian Paintbrush (Buffalo Press 2020)

Cover Art: Steven Schroeder
Book Design: Rowan Kehn

Turning Plow Press

ISBN: 978-1-7355762-1-3

Praise for *Too Late for Manly Hands*

When I was first privileged to hear Hank Jones read his poems many years ago during the Langdon Literary Review Weekend art and literary festival in Granbury, Texas, I knew he was a poet of extraordinary power and promise. The poems he selected for this book, his first published collection of poetry, certainly solidify my initial impression of his work.

The opening poem of the book is representative of many poems he dedicates to a razor-sharp exploration of domestic relationships, especially those of father/son and husband/wife. With uncanny insight and skilled manipulation of language, he captures the dichotomy of terror and love which characterizes so many father/son dynamics: the strict discipline meted out by a military father juxtaposed with an unrequited longing for warmth and affection. Equally impressive are the poems he dedicates to his wife and her grueling recovery from the ravages of serious cancer. The simple, direct diction employed by Jones in each and every poem belies the richness of his erudite allusions: from Zen to Tolstoy and Bach's *Cello Suites* to Beethoven's *Late String Quartets*.

In short, this collection is a rare first book of poetry, infused with heart and wisdom, the heart of raw emotional honesty and the hard-earned wisdom of a life fully realized.

Larry D. Thomas
Member, Texas Institute of Letters
2008 Texas State Poet Laureate

I've known Hank Jones for a few years now, heard him read his work in different venues around Oklahoma and Texas and never doubted this book was coming one day. And at last, it's here, and well worth the wait. It is Hank to the core: sensitive, funny, intelligent, and incredibly honest. What you won't find here is the stuff the televangelist in Hank's poem, "Be a Cannibal for the Lord" is offering – the usual shit, not here, I guarantee it.

In "More Life to Lead, More Books to Read," he declares, "The only thing I ever wanted was to be a poet"; well, mi amigo you got it. You put the words together, just right. You made me laugh. You made me cry. You moved me to feel human. I love this book.

Ron Wallace,
Winner of the 2018 Oklahoma Book Award
for *Renegade and Other Poems*

Table of Contents

Table of Contents (cont.)

For Julie,

without whom there would be no poems,
there would be no book.

Close Kin

There's a tree, a rather magnificent cedar tree
grown tall and mighty over the old farmhouse
but the main trunk split in its growth,
sending two scissor arms high into the sky.

And one of these offshoots has spread its branches over the house;
beautiful, yes, and providing necessary shade to the sunny side of the house,
but the ice storms we get these years suggest the house is in danger of fallen limbs.
At least this is what my father thinks, and the reason he, my brother,
and I are out here this late autumn morning.

We fire up the chainsaws and tractor and commence to whittle the tree down
and away from its encroachment on this hundred-year-old house
where my father and most of his brothers and sisters were born.
It's a day's work as we begin by cutting the upper limbs off,
careful to avoid any falling on the house.

When we've got a big enough pile of brush,
we load it in the tractor's bucket and make a run to the burn pile.
We talk some, but largely work in silence.

Early on we lose the overshirts, and when the sun is high
we begin to sweat. But we feel good
using our bodies and our strength and agility
to swing the chainsaws up at awkward angles
using our geometric eye to ensure the limbs fall where they ought.

We lose ourselves in the work, stopping occasionally for water,
and for lunch at noon, because it's not long till the sun is going behind Chalk Mountain,
and dusk finds us with the offending limb cut down to size.

The tree now looks unnaturally formed, with one mighty limb ascending to the north,
and only empty space where its brother limb was ten hours ago.
The ground is littered with sawdust from our labors,
the thick smoke of the oil/gas mix hangs heavy in the air.

We remove our sweat-stained gloves and observe our handiwork.
We've done well, succeeded in bringing the cedar tree into alignment with our desire.
I feel a deep pleasure at the work we've done together, at the silent bond
we've shared as we tackled something bigger than ourselves,

but it is tinged also with a sharp sadness. Caught up in our masculine endeavor,
I never questioned whether this was the right thing to do,
only picked up tools with my closest kin and made the world ours.

1

Digging a Grave

I helped dig a grave with some ranchers
one of whose boys had died.
Mentally disabled, he had drowned in a swimming pool
when everyone else looked away.
The father, in his grief,
built his son's casket of unfinished pine,
then we joined him to dig the grave.
There were eight or ten of us, boys and men,
taking turns with a metal rod to break up the
hard New Mexico soil,
then one by one, we'd jump in the hole
and shovel out dirt
until our muscles ached
and we could no longer
lift the dirt-full shovel.
Then another would take a turn,
digging down as the hole got deeper.
Before too long, we were over our heads in the grave,
six by four.
It occurred to me as I worked
that this is the right way
to bury someone you love:
ache and sweat out the grief,
as the blisters form on your uncalloused hands.

The Lost Art of Whittling

I was given my first pocketknife
at Nogal Mesa Ranchmen's Camp Meeting
where the old men sat around
between church services and whittled
pieces of wood, usually discarded branch,
into child-delighting shapes:
a horse, a pistol, a rifle, a mountain lion,
or, my favorite, a little wooden four-barred cage
with a wooden ball inside.

The ball freed, as if by magic,
from the wood itself,
rolled up and down the bars.
There was even a tiny hole in the top for a string
that you could hang from your belt
or from the awning of the travel trailer we slept in,
or even from a Christmas tree, come the right time of year.

I stood, a child watching whittling men
wield sharp-edged knives
as juniper shavings peeled and curled
under strong hand's command
around scuffed and dirt-stained boots
of rancher and cowboy,
who, godlike, made dull matter
take shape, find form.

First Rifle

I got my first rifle, a .22, at the age of 8
and was informed that I was no longer to play with guns.
If I was old enough to carry a real rifle,
then guns were no longer toys.

I accepted that rifle with all the seriousness expected of me:
a rite of passage into the world of men.
I practiced my aim on cans and cardboard targets,
but soon moved on to jackrabbits and cottontails,
and the occasional bird.

I remember shooting at a cottontail one time,
my father looking on and me desperate to impress.
I aimed carefully, fired, the ping of the .22
a mixture of soft exhalation with hard-edged pop underneath.

The rabbit had gone frozen at our approach,
as rabbits are wont to do when they feel a threat.
And it stood frozen still, despite the noise of the shot
and my apparent miss. I loaded another bullet and fired again.

The rabbit remained as before, no movement at all
save the almost imperceptible breathing in and out.
I fired again, then again,
and still the rabbit sat there.

I may have missed with one or another shot,
but certainly not with all.
After eight shots, my father moved forward to investigate
and the rabbit never moved.

Perhaps it jerked finally when my father came near it,
but I had indeed shot true and the rabbit's movement
was a wounded lurch that did not take it to safety.

My father was upon it, and to my amazement and my horror,
he took his boot and crushed the rabbit's skull.
Up to this point all my murders had been done cleanly,
with bullets, and I never had to watch an animal suffer long.

But this was a new kind of death to me,
this the brutal death of the weak and defenseless by the all-powerful.
Here the rabbit was no longer pristine in its natural beauty
with only a few streaks of blood to mark where the bullet had done its work.

Instead the rabbit's head was crushed into the dust,
all misshapen with jelly eyes lusterless in strange asymmetry.
How can I explain the strange feeling I had then,
torn by an inchoate recognition for the first time of the fallen world.

Charles Manson and Me

Cavalier, North Dakota. I was six or so,
Mom was away, I'm not sure where,
Dad was busy doing dad things.
I got to watching *Helter Skelter*, I don't remember how.
But I do remember the whole damn movie, even now,
seared into my brain like I was one of Charlie's clan,
listening to one of Charlie's rants.
I remember him making a bus fly
that didn't really fly.
I remember all the blood and all the screaming,
Die Pigs scrawled in blood on the walls,
which I could read all by myself.
I remember the hyper-intense eyes of the man
pretending to be Manson,
as he glowered at everyone,
then stared into the camera,
and looked right at me.
When they finally hauled him away,
the swastika already carved in his forehead,
the most chilling thing happened.
The movie ended with the remarkable statement
that Charles Manson was due for parole in seven years.
I could read, I could do math,
If the movie was set in 1969,
the year of my birth,
then seven years, like my birthday,
was right around the corner.
I don't think anything has ever terrified me as much as that.
A terror I had to keep to myself
because I was watching something I shouldn't have been watching.
The windows were suddenly filled with the moving shadows
of bald women with rolling eyes,
so I slipped into the kitchen and found the biggest, scariest knife I could find,
hid it under my pillow
somehow managing to sleep on it without slitting my own throat.
I don't remember my mother ever saying anything to me
about the kitchen knife she must have found one morning
while changing the sheets on my bed.

P.S.—Mom has since told me she once found a paring knife under my pillow.

Watching *Huck Finn* with Father, circa 1976

Imagine a boy out with his stiff military father
without the soft mother to run interference.
The father, in civilian clothes, still
stands straight, moves rigidly, as if on parade,
the young son tries to do the same.

They go to the theater, sit in the plush, worn seats,
to see a new version of *Huckleberry Finn*
because the boy loved the Tom Sawyer he'd seen once on TV,
is eager now to watch Tom's best friend on his own adventure,
hopes for a glimpse of the wild Tom, hair flying, feet dirty,
the boy whom no force of man could manage to control.

He watches now the wilder Huck, wilder hair, dirtier feet,
breaking the laws of his society
to help his friend Jim escape from a terrible fate.
He's moved beyond words by Huck when he sees
Jim's blood and says, "Why, your blood's red just like mine,"
and Jim replies that he is a man and what else did Huck expect.

Somehow this most human of moments
causes this boy, desperate to be a man for his father,
to weep uncontrollably for the rest of the picture
while the stern father sits beside him uncomfortably
with no idea at all what to do.

Genesis 19:30-38

At age ten, desirous of being a good Christian
I set myself the task of reading the Bible
from cover to cover.

Taking the giant family book
bound in white calf skin, gilt-edged,
renaissance cherubim and seraphim
dancing round the cover,

I opened the heavy tome
and began to read.

The creation stories I knew well,
and the garden tale
with snakes and breasts.

I plowed on through Abel and Cain,
and Noah and his Ark,
Abraham killing his son, then not,
mostly surprised at how short these stories were
that had always stood so tall in church sermon.

But what brought me to a screeching halt
was the story of Sodom and Gomorrah,
and not because those fabled sin cities
were destroyed in fire and brimstone.
This much I knew well.

But it was Lot and his daughters,
fleeing the burning cities,
that ruined the Bible for me for all time.

I was prepared for Lot's wife—
the one who couldn't leave sin behind—
to turn to salt, always vaguely convinced she
somehow deserved it, though little in the text confirmed that.

No, it was when Lot's daughters got him drunk
and lay with him, I think that was the word used,
that I had to stop. Even my naive ten-year-old self
knew what laid really meant.

I didn't know, still don't, what to do with that,
Lot, one of the good guys, doing something
that only the worst would do,
and for this transgression,
not only not getting turned to salt,
nor destroyed by fire from the heavens,

but just getting himself off
with his daughters,

and nary a peep from You Know Who.

What I Learned in Boy Scouts

Well, there was the time the scout from Spain
told us how to fuck a cat
giving us a visual as his hands
pretended to hold two back legs
as he pulled the yowling creature
onto his stiff adolescent prick.

Or the time the scout from England
showed us what an uncircumcised penis looked like,
its hooded glory in marked contrast to our German helmets.

Or the dirty jokes told around the campfire
late at night after the adults had gone to bed,
with punchlines like, "Ding-dong, dammit. Ding-dong," and "Shh! They 'bout to land."

Or how to put a fire out by pissing on it,
giant white plume rising into the night sky,
smell of ammoniac embers burning the nose,
strange disinclination to cook over said fire the morning after.

But also how to build a fire with no more than two matches,
how to tie knots like an old-time sailor,
how to lash poles together to build towers,
and, at least in theory, a bridge.
How to put up and break down camp,
how to pack forty pounds in a pack
and carry it entire days,
living, mostly, on only what you can carry on your back.

Or canoeing for days down a filthy river
with nasty white foam washing off of the farm fields we passed
ensuring we paddled our canoes carefully
so as not to end up next to it.

Or how to sleep under a billion stars,
the shy Milky Way standing out clearly
to my eyes away from city lights for the first time.

Or the total silence of a forest night with no human noise
except the tiny bit we brought.

Something Lost in a Cheap Motel Room in Las Cruces, New Mexico

A family of four shares a room to save money,
but the two teenage boys feel awkward sharing a bed.
The TV's on as one by one they all fall asleep
except for the oldest boy who's
transfixed by a movie.
He doesn't even know its name
but it stars a young Jan Michael Vincent
as a wild, tough country boy,
much like what our young viewer wishes he could be.
And this young man in the movie
wants so bad to get laid
but his pretty girlfriend just won't give it up,
so he turns to this big, dumb country girl who's
rumored to be easy.
And she is, and our young hero gets his.
But then a peculiar thing happens: he falls for her.
He falls hard for her, and pretty soon he's
running around like she's his number one girl,
and this just doesn't sit right with anybody.
I mean, the whole town turns on him
but because he's too tough to fuck with
and won't take shit off anyone,
they go for his girl, the easy one, the big dumb one.
And you see, this boy's buddies,
his best friends, from childhood and all that,
they think they need to save him,
and they decide they can best do that
by reminding him that every boy in those parts
has gone to his gal to lose his virginity,
or to get some easy tail when the sap's up,
so they go to her, and every one of them has had her before,
and they expect to have her again, but she's
different now, prettier, carries herself with something like dignity,
and she tells them where to get off.
They don't take this well: they're sore at their friend
cause he's violated some sacred code that no one even understands,
they're sore at her because they are, after all, horny,
and she's the only sure thing they had,
and they're just sore in general and figure someone's got to pay.
And it will be her.
So they rape her, all of them, all his friends.
There's not much left when our young hero finds her
but he knows exactly what happened
and he knows exactly what he'll do,

11

so he goes where he knows he'll find them
at the pool hall, around a table.
He marches in and his buddies look nonchalantly at him,
like, what's up,
and before they can see the murder in his eyes,
he's started whacking them with a pool cue,
and not just to hurt, but to kill,
and one of the friends, the goofy one that everyone likes,
but who raped her right alongside the others,
starts screaming like a girl, just this
high-pitched wail, as he watches his friend
kill his friends and knows his time is coming
and right then, at this highest point of the drama
the young teenager watching this movie in a motel bed,
staring incredulously at the realest movie he's
ever seen up to this point in his life,
dying to know what's going to happen next,
is suddenly pulled out of his intense concentration
by his father who's been awakened by the high-pitched screaming
and who says roughly, even brutally, *turn that off now!*
And the eldest son knows there's no arguing the point,
no way to explain that he has to know what happens next,
that it's basically the most important thing in the entire world
that he sees how this ends, and he doesn't know the title,
and this is the age before the Internet,
so basically if he turns it off now,
he'll never ever know how this will end,
but none of that matters, the order's been given,
the TV goes off and the young man
lies in the sudden pitch black
and feels the most intense hatred for his father,
but also the intensest kind of loss at being
sucked into a story completely
and then being jerked out of it at the point where all the truth
a story can muster was about to be revealed,
and he lies there in that dark and feels a profound sadness
like he's just lost something infinitely precious
that he's not likely to find again.

Touch and Go

The boy is learning to fly solo, practicing touch and go's
as the father looks on from below, proud of his son, but nervous,
wondering how much trust you should put in a fifteen-year-old pilot.

The boy circles the airport and sticks the landing a bit hard,
but the plane's tough, bounces and speeds up for another take off,
once again graceful as it lifts and glides into a turn,
lifting and turning around the landing strip
as it makes its way back for another touch down.

This time, though, clouds have moved in
and the father loses the plane in the sculpted whiteness.
The father, a pilot too, knows what the son is up against,
the vertigo and misdirection that can happen
lost in clouds. The father could panic, but what good would it do?

So he stares at the far end of a cloud and prays a tiny plane appears.
He waits and waits and time drags on, much longer
than it seems it should take for the plane to re-appear.
Just at the point when he's started to talk to God,
started to make promises about what he'll do, what he'll give up,
if that plane will just appear,

there it is, right where it's supposed to be.
It eases into the final descent, ailerons coming down
to slow the plane into the final drop to the runaway
and the plane lands, smooth this time,
like this boy's been landing planes for twenty years.

When the practice is over, the plane taxis to its parking spot,
the boy emerges, the father keeps himself from running to him.

"I lost you in that cloud bank for a bit. How'd it go up there?"
The boy, unaware his father was watching the whole time,
confesses that it was a bit rough today.
"How'd you know when to turn for the landing? You couldn't see anything up there."
"Oh," the boy replies, "I knew how long it was supposed to take
before I turned, so I just counted it out and turned when I usually do."

The boy walks off to finish signing out the plane.
The father walks behind, a new respect for his strange son.
The boy grows up, leaves flying behind,
forgets this incident ever took place.
The father remembers it for thirty-five years,
and one day, over a game of dominos,
tells a group that includes his grown son

about the time he watched as his boy was lost to him in the heavens
and he stood, powerless on the ground,
waiting for his son to return.

In the Buddha's Belly

I'd taken a handful of Boy Scouts on a hike
following trails pounded by thousands of feet
past ancient trees, never quite sure the path we were on
would get us there.

But we arrived at the temple in Kamakura,
stood in awe of the giant Buddha in his greenish tint
from his five hundred years in Japanese rains.

I walked inside the Buddha, the boys behind.
Having read a few books on Zen, I knelt
and began to breathe in and out from the diaphragm.

No one else was in there, just me and a few boys
whom I'd forgotten about.

When it came back to my mind that I
was responsible for these young lives
following me about in a strange country,
I opened my eyes with a start, and found them all

kneeling in the same posture as me,
faces forward, breathing slowly,
perfectly at peace in the Buddha's belly.

Kind of Blue

It's like the song's trying to find itself
walking down this dark alley
that suddenly opens up into a chorus
of angels who are
holding out hands and pulling
you toward them

> *Jazz came into my life through a girl,*
> *the most beautiful girl I ever knew.*
> *It took me a year to win her love,*
> *a year to lose it.*

and before you know it,
damn it, you just start to fly
and it's like you move your feet
and they're wings and with
the slightest motion

> *She introduced me to jazz. Jazz*
> *is revered in Japan. The Japanese,*
> *at least those who listen, love jazz*
> *more than they love almost anything*
> *else. And though this girl wasn't*
> *Japanese, she'd grown up there, and*
> *absorbed what was cool in Japan,*
> *and what was cool in Japan was jazz.*

I'm floating through the
shimmering air and the clouds
part and I'm heading toward
the sun, but the sun's shine
doesn't hurt my eyes at all,

> *So when I lost this girl after*
> *my first year of college,*
> *I tried to find anything I could*
> *find that would keep me tied to her,*
> *that would, somehow, make me cool*
> *enough for her to love again.*

it's like I'm looking into an
ocean of salty tears that
soothe my eyes and wash away
all the dirty grime that many
years on the sooty earth have
left layered there

> *And so I bought a book on the*
> *hundred greatest jazz albums,*
> *went to a record store in Austin,*
> *and bought the album that everyone*
> *said was the greatest jazz album*
> *ever recorded. And that was*
> Kind of Blue.

and I realize I've
been blind for years and
can finally see. Maybe I
was born blind, but I'm not blind
anymore.

> *And then I fell in love*
> *with jazz. And though I never*
> *got that girl back again, I*
> *got something better, something that*
> *no one could ever take away*
> *from me again. I got jazz.*

And I see everything—
all the world and all
its people, and animals, and
trees and it's all
crystal clear and clean
and everything just flows
like water, streams
like sunlight.

I Think I Hated Every Day I Played Football

I take my dog out to pee at 6:30 in the morning
and I can already hear the coaches' whistles
coming from the practice fields,
can even hear the geeks in band practicing already
to cheer these young warriors on to victory
or defeat. It was the Buddha who said to leave victory behind,
because the defeated live in pain.

It was always missing in me, the aggressiveness,
the necessary killer instinct you have to have
to really be good at football, or wrestling,
or maybe any sport.

I hated the grueling, repetitive practices,
had no capacity to really hit hard the way some guys do,
that last-moment acceleration
right before impact
when they hit you so hard your head literally rings.

I think I always did the opposite,
at the last minute recoiling from the blow,
no real desire on my part to hit or be hit,
something like the way in a race I'd always look back
to see my competitor,
slowing down if necessary for them to catch up,
always losing the race in the process.

Maybe I was Buddhist long before I met Buddha,
though the Christ I love would be no football player either,
too busy turning cheeks and washing feet
to worry about laying a smack-down on someone.

They claim they taught us discipline, leadership,
perseverance, character.
What I remember is blindly doing
what everyone else was doing,
even when deep down I hated it,
following the orders of grown men
because they were mean and barked loudly,
enjoying the glow that comes from doing the expected thing,
walking around like tiny gods,
cheered on by short-skirted girls and brass and drums
and mobs of crowds yelling wildly in unison
to kill, kill, kill.

Zen vs. a Texas Summer

Nineteen, freshly heartbroken,
weary of the human world, and seeking
a deeper mystical understanding of the universe,
I formed a vague desire to be one with nature.
Dressing as close to naked as I could manage
wearing only tank top, short shorts, flip-flops,

I drove out to our leased ranch, a few stringy cows grazing,
down a faded dirt road till the road disappeared,
then walked till I couldn't see my car anymore,
couldn't hear anything but birdsong and cow-grunt.
I found a cedar tree to sit under in the dirt,
pulled out *Zen and the Art of Motorcycle Maintenance*,
and tried to get lost in philosophical journeying.

The sweat began dripping in my eyes almost immediately
as a thousand cicadas resumed their unholy screech,
a horsefly buzzed, looking for
purchase on my exposed soft skin,
a pesky mosquito droned in my damp ear,
and a fire ant crawled up my leg and bit me.

I realized, in an instant of enlightenment,
the futility of contemplation in a Texas summer,
as mind succumbed to flesh, flesh to nature.

My Season in Hell

> *Ah! I've been through too much . . . let me rip out these few ghastly pages from my notebook of the damned.*
> *–Arthur Rimbaud, "A Season in Hell"*

I stick my hands in each pocket, looking
for things that stain, shred
or otherwise derail the process:

pocket change, lipstick, nails,
      wads of paper, chewing gum,
           odd bits of this and that . . .
cologne, perfume, sweat,
      blood, urine, feces, cum . . .

Buttons on the left side in one pile,
      buttons on the right in another,
           $1.50 for a shirt, $2.75 for a blouse,

pants, skirts, dresses, suits, neckties, scarves . . .

As long as the front door is open,
      the piles never shrink:
search the pockets, tag the stains, put them in piles,
      again and again and again.

I start to look at customers with hate,
      but it's a job, and it's the easy one,
keeps me out of the burning pits
      of perchloroethylene hell

where the unlucky ones live,
      stooped over steaming presses
perpetually from dark to midday
      when it'll be so hot outside, leaving hell will be no relief.

The difference between me and those stuck in the back
      is that I'm young and a college student,
           and this is a part-time job,
and someday I'll leave this place behind forever,

but they'll remain until drugs or alcohol or immigration
      or some crime as yet unpunished

will sink them lower than they already are
       as they labor to make us unwrinkled and stain-free.

So I'm Talking to This English Girl

So I'm talking to this English girl,
Oxford-educated, beautiful, young.
Shit, she's got it all. We're talking literature
and I'm doing my best to impress her.
She says at one point, "There are some writers you
have to read everything they wrote to really understand them."
I agree, and start racking my brain, going over all the books I've read...
Surely there's some damn author I've read all the works of,
at least some damn guy who didn't write too much.
Salinger comes to mind, but dammit,
I never finished *Raise High the Roofbeam, Carpenter*.
So I'm coming up with nothing when she says, "You know, like Tolstoy."
And I give up right there. Just flat give up.

Be a Cannibal for the Lord

Based on a story told to me by Joey Brown

The wife was away and I passed the time
dolorous before the tv
when my dog sat on the remote
and discovered a televangelist.

As I reached to change the channel
I was struck by something
the slick-haired man said:
You must, he said, be a cannibal for the Lord.

And I was stunned
as I released the control and flopped back on the couch,
pondering these bizarre and shocking words.

We must be cannibals for the Lord!

Yes, I thought,
rather than smugly, glibly, apathetically
just eating and drinking our Lord,

this man was saying we must eat each other!
Or maybe that wasn't what he was saying,
but I struggled with this fascinating new angle on religion,

wondered briefly how on earth
it would bring in any money for Reverend Slick standing there,
but in love with the metaphorical possibilities.

And that's where I was when the wife returned,
a look of shock and horror on her face at what she
caught me watching,

as I blushed as if caught masturbating.

I quickly explained what Rev. Slick had said,
saw her step back in confusion
and mild, glimmering interest.

Then we both turned to the screen
as the preacher said again,
this time more clearly,
"You must all be accountable to the Lord."

And my heart fell, and my wife smirked,
as I realized that this dude wasn't saying anything new,
just the usual shit.

Somewhere between Belief and Disbelief

I'm not particularly religious.
Hell, I might be an atheist.
But my upbringing in the church
sings in me still.
The story of the Good Samaritan,
the Sermon on the Mount,
the dictums to help the least of these,
to love your enemy as yourself,
are part of my fiber and being.
I still find myself occasionally
asking God for guidance,
praying silently to myself
not my will, but thine, be done,
thinking, sometimes,
that God is with me,
asking, God be with me,
and a voice replies,
God is with me,

thanking God when some
unexpected blessing comes my way:
the cop gives me a warning
instead of a ticket,
the tire goes flat in the driveway
instead of the highway,
the car runs out of gas next to a gas station,
a stranger shows an unexpected kindness,
smiling when I was feeling inexplicably blue,
or opens a door I couldn't find,
my loved one's suffering
is lessened or relieved
when neither seemed possible.

There is a design to our lives, says Hamlet,
rough hew them how we will,
and sometimes I believe him.
But then I wake up again in Trump's America,
and have a hard time
believing in anything at all.
Am reminded yet again
that the world isn't right,
that the innocent suffer,
that my life is not worth
the tears of one child,

and with Ivan Karamazov,
I respectfully hand back my ticket.

A nonbeliever caught between the wish to believe
and the despair that there's nothing to believe in,
I dangle here in my disbelief,
resisting.

Friday, 8 December 2017

I read about prisoners at Guantanamo
creating stunning pieces of art out of almost nothing,
such as a ship built of cardboard and t-shirt fibers
because a ship can escape,
because Noah saved life on earth with a ship,

but when the art gets too much attention,
when trapped souls nestle in the smallest part of a blue sky,
the works are confiscated, archived or destroyed,
what's the difference.

I try to remind myself that if I someday am imprisoned,
my soul being crushed by powers I am powerless against,
that I will remember to create something beautiful
with the materials I find around me

because this is how the soul speaks to other souls.
Perhaps it's the only way.

As if this line of thought weren't dark enough,
the next thing I run across is a video
about a polar bear starving to death.

The photographer said he wanted to capture what climate change really looks like.

So I watch this video, watch
this magnificent creature,
white fur still beautiful as it hangs off
what's left of the skeleton inside

as this tired, worn creature digs in human trash for any sustenance,
finds none in our leavings, stumbles a few feet away,
lays down in a weary wait for death.

And I'm left here in my kitchen,
knowing the distractions of the day
will carry me far away from thinking on such things.

But I don't want that to happen,
I don't want to forget men who've been imprisoned
for sixteen years without charge,
don't want to forget the image of a polar bear starving to death,

But I will forget these things as I blindly move through my day.
As if imprisonment and starvation could never, will never happen to me.
As if there is nothing I can do to help those suffering right now, today, this moment.

As if there's nothing I could do.

A View of Life through the Lens of Cancer

You were always going to die
but you didn't know when
and that was the gift
though you didn't know it.

Because when you're told you're going to die
and you can see that place in the not too distant future
that doesn't include you

it has the effect of ruining everything.

The beautiful day with its green grass and sunshine,
blue sky and birds calling,

brings no comfort,
seems designed for someone else's joy.

No music that doesn't sound tinny,
no movie that doesn't seem false,
no words that get up and dance,

they just lie there
lifeless on the white page

as they must always have done.

Piano Pain

The piano playing is painful,
grating against the grain
of my mournful mood.

Cheerful and chipper
the terrible tune turns
my stomach sour

in this lobby I long to leave.
But I must wait withering
inside for you to emerge

with the needless news
of what we already know:
the cancer recurs.

Waiting on the PET Scan

The tech invites me back
to sit with Julie.

He tells me she's emitting
a little radiation though
so I can't sit too close.

I tell him I'll call her sunshine
and take my chances.

Life on Pause

That's what it felt like,
these past ten months
as we struggled through
chemo, surgery, radiation.

I say "we," but all I did was
stand on the side and watch.

"Bolero" and a Train

Ravel's "Bolero" is on the radio
when we get stopped in Cresson
by the train.

Our thirty-third trip to and from Ft. Worth,
daily but for weekends and, for some reason, Presidents' Day.

This is our last trip,
your radiation treatment done,
the last hurdle in our long journey
from cancer to cancer-free.

Inexplicably, this is our first train in all that time.
We got stopped by it heading in,
and now, heading back, here it is again.

"Bolero" is the perfect tune as the train moves slowly
one direction, stops, then moves slowly in reverse.

My favorite part is when you can see the end
of the train coming,
but it slows slowly down and stops,
still blocking the highway,
and then just as slowly reverses course.

It's done that twice now as "Bolero" builds and gets louder,
but never resolves,
just repeats itself *ad nauseum*.

Once we might have thought
ourselves trapped in some kind of hell,
while a train moved forward and back endlessly,
while "Bolero" mounted in obnoxious repetition.

But after all we've been through,
this is only an amusingly absurd sideshow
entertaining us briefly
as we wait patiently to get home.

Middle-Aged Aubade

Rain on the roof sloshing
seamlessly through gutters,
wind moving through trees holding
doggedly on to a few remaining leaves,
chimes on our backporch ringing
in exquisite, meaningless harmonies,
birds anxiously twittering,
perhaps over scarce food, or cold, or rain.

The first gleam of morning
gradually lightens our windows
as I snuggle deeper under covers
next to my partner, squeezing my eyes shut,
resisting, for a while longer,
this as yet unwelcome autumn day.

But the dog begins to grumble
and snort her morning announcement
that she's ready to be let out,
as the cats agitate against the closed door
for their first munchies of the day.

The unpleasant sounds of you
blowing your nose and me passing gas
suggest that sleep and amorousness
have flitted sneakily off together
leaving us to morning rituals
as we make our way to breakfast
and the unavoidable, beautiful day.

Wild Ride

I put the towel beneath her belly, hoist her backend
and we're off, waterskiing across the backyard.
I hold on tightly as my old dog follows the worn path
she has wormed through our yard, almost twelve years
walking the same circumference
with occasional forays to the center to poop or pee.
I am now her hind legs, a poor substitute,
that hobbles behind as I try not to hobble her.

Crippled now for twelve days, we don't know what to do.
Her four hundred-dollar wheelchair proves too cumbersome:
by the time she's strapped in, her heart's gone out of it,
and dull eyed she stares at us, questioning her torture.

But when I get the towel under her, off she goes,
a one-dog team of bucking horses eager to pull the load.
She slips into her old ways, sniffs the air like she's always done
before heading out to sniff her yard, put together the pieces
of the story of what's happened since last she investigated,
what squirrels, what birds had the audacity to challenge her domain,
checking the perimeter once more for the ten-thousandth time
to be sure no threats are lurking.

Then it's back in the house to the pad where she'll lie
mostly inert, eager enough for the biscuits and water I give her,
before she slumps down, wondering when
I'll take her on the next wild ride.

The Murder of the Chair

I look carefully up and down the street to be sure no neighbors are watching.

The chair has sat in our garage our entire time together, worn out, dirty, nothing but foam where the seat should be.

My wife always said she would get it re-covered, that it was her favorite chair, no other chair ever as comfortable to read in, to nap in.

How could I know if she was right? The chair, as long as I'd known it, was never in a fit state for companionship.

Our big move north to a beautiful but much smaller house means that many things have not made the cut.

We hauled trailer load after trailer load to our new home, to a storage shed, to the dump.

I'm alone at the old home now, with what little that's left, some of which will go with me north, some of which will be given away, the rest will be shoved in our green bin and hauled off.

The chair had survived all previous attempts to discard it. My wife, sweet, sentimental heart, could not part with it.

And so it's sat there, in the garage, while objects around it are slowly thinned away.

I don't know what to do with it. I'm tired of looking at it. It's in my way. I'm constantly moving it here or there, putting things on it, taking things away.

Tomorrow is trash day, the bin is still half empty. Today, I decided, is the day.

I pull out my sawzall, not sure if I should use the wood blade or the metal, go with wood.

I start to cut into the chair. It doesn't make a sound. It doesn't even whimper. Just stoically takes all I give it.

I go for an arm first, hit some staples and maybe a nail, but I get it cut. Have to use a box cutter blade to cut the old fabric, though it mostly falls apart. I take the other arm.

Then I go for the wingback. I go down the middle, and it falls apart like inverted wings taking flight but in opposite directions toward the ground.

The seat and legs prove toughest of all. I try a middle cut, but it's full of complicated springs that get in my blade's way. I contemplate a metal blade, but decide to cut around the springs. I have to take my box cutter to split what's left of the old, dirty fabric. It doesn't want to give. I almost slice myself trying to get it cut, as if my blood might be required for this sacrifice.

But I get it cut, and split into four or five or six pieces, which barely fit in the bin, but they fit.

I glance up and down the street to see if there have been any witnesses.

I shove the chair in the bin, but a leg and part of a wing are sticking out. I push the bin into the garage to hide the dismembered body until tomorrow morning, when I'll sneak it out early before the sun has risen to reveal all of the past night's sins.

I clean up the mess on the ground, staples, fabric, foam, bits of wood. I look once more up and down the street, satisfy myself no one saw the deed, close the garage door, head inside to clean up.

I'm sweating like I just ran a mile. I look into the mirror as I lather my hands. I'm surprised to see the brow locked in furrow, the eyes a bit mad and desperate.

I look as if I'd just committed a murder. I feel a strange sort of guilt. The chair was more complicated than I could have imagined. It was no simple chair. It was a feat of engineering.

And without so much as a goodbye, I slaughtered the thing to rid myself of detritus, to clear my space of an eyesore, to move on to the dump something I was no longer willing to take responsibility for.

It will be gone tomorrow. All evidence erased. I'll tell my wife someone took it, so she'll sleep easier thinking the chair found someone to appreciate it, as she had always done.

I'll bury my guilt. I'll tell myself it was for the best. That I was at the end of my rope with this move and something had to go. We live in a culture of waste. I've thrown away many things that gave me a twinge, for their perceived value, for the massive waste buried beneath us and flushed into our oceans. I'll get over this.

But it nags me. And I'll probably write about it, and probably read it somewhere, and then my wife will know the truth.

It's the Dandelions That Give Us Away

If not for those damned insouciant yellow buttonheads,
those straightly tall runners with their white fuzzy heads,
our neighbors might almost forget how strange we are,
might almost think we're like them.

I mean there's not a blade of grass out there,
it's all weeds, but most of our weedy bouquets have the courtesy to lay low,
so that only close inspection, the kind only walkers or salesmen
would be close enough to render, gives us away.

I mean, it's not a pretty yard,
because we are loath to use poisons and chemical fertilizers
and too much water, which seem to be
the only ways to raise a lawn in this harsh Texas landscape.

But I'll concede to the neighbors here one day,
do my part not to give in to total alienation
from what is after all our local community,
and I'll drag the mower out, fire it up, and slay those dandelion upstarts.

Well, we all know cutting the heads off hardly kills a dandelion,
so I'll look forward, in a day to two, to their rebel yell
again spread yellow across the yard.

Mosquito

I think I could make peace with a mosquito
if she'd just take a bit of my blood and go about her business.
I mean, I have Buddhist proclivities, don't like killing anything,
and if the damn mosquito would just take a dainty sip and move on,
I'd say, go in peace, little sister, living's a hard road for all us,
take what you need and go.

A Rash of Children

I'm sitting in the doctor's office lobby,
childless but surrounded by children,
a rash erupting in vague patches everywhere on my body.

If I had kids, we'd all be here today after our weekend on the river,
my children inheritors of my propensity to break out
in a rash if I look at poison ivy.

Almost fifty, I've probably denied myself the knowledge
of procreating and reproducing tiny versions of myself
to run around in circles at my feet.

My friend Walter, unmarried, no children, told me once
about an affair with a beautiful, married Korean student
who became pregnant with his child, and had to have an abortion

before she could return to her home country,
to her waiting, unaware husband.
Walter died a few years after this, leaving almost nothing behind.

I wonder if in that realm he now resides
he regrets there's not a child here who bears some trace of him.
I wonder if I'll regret, someday, my own choice not to have children.

Right now, as I sit here itching, waiting to be squeezed in,
I think I'd rather have my poison ivy rash,
which at least can be cured and will only trouble me a short while.

Forgetting How to Run

I swore I'd never forget how to run fast,
the way young boys do playing catch,
feet moving so fast at times they hardly seem to touch ground.

I remember watching my father play a game of softball
when he was about the age I am now.
A natural homerun hitter, he swung at a bad pitch
and had to run like hell to first.
I remember the strange embarrassment I felt
watching this strong man run as hard as he could
on legs that seemed somehow out of sync
with his upper body,
a movement that reminded me somehow
of a fish trying to swim on dry land.

I swore then, an inarticulate pledge,
that I wouldn't let myself forget how to run,
wouldn't let my body lose the natural feel
of running like wind barely breaking the surface of water.

Imagine my chagrin to reach my middle forties,
trapped most days of the year in a small, squat, windowless office,
and realize I haven't run like a boy in what must be close to a decade.

And I realize now how old age gets you:
not a hard, vicious frontal assault,
the kind I was prepared for,
but a slowly creeping insinuation,
so slow it might as well be creeping death,
that moves in and becomes you so subtly,
you never even see the change in the mirror.

Just one day you run into a guy you knew twenty years ago
and he tells you how fat you've become
and you go back to that mirror,
look closely, and a middle-aged man
who reminds you strangely of your father,
stares back at you.

And you put on your shorts and tired running shoes
and head outside to prove it isn't so,
and your confident walk becomes a hesitant jog
that somehow won't kick into a full-bore run,
as your legs and upper body send messages to your brain
claiming that communication has broken down somewhere,
somewhere around where your manhood is supposed to be.

Playing Catch before the Game

We arrive early, pop the tailgate,
finish the bottle of sake from the sushi restaurant
the night before. It warms us in the unusual late-spring chill,
gets us ready for our game of catch before
the Rangers/A's game begins.

It's been probably twenty years since I last played catch,
my glove is stiff, my arm rubbery.
I miss balls thrown my way, closing the mitt too soon,
or misjudge slightly the ball's descent.
When I throw, it's like I'm using someone else's arm
sewn onto my body, not quite the right fit.
It twists at strange angles as I extend into the release,
the ball seldom going where I want it to.

But Paul, my best friend, and his son, PJ,
are good sports and happy to be out here playing catch.
PJ, the youngster, just turned thirteen,
is the one who gets most of my bad throws,
sending him across the parking lot
as the hard baseball rolls unimpeded
as far as momentum will take it,
PJ gamely in pursuit, never complaining,
just retrieving the ball and tossing it skyward
toward his father.

Fortunately, the Rangers are bad this year,
the A's too,
so the parking lot fills slowly,
and there are precious few witnesses
to our rather sad game of catch.
It means we can just enjoy the silliness
of grown men and a growing boy
throwing a hard ball into leather gloves
as if this were all there was in the world to do
as the day gradually darkens
and we stop to have a beer from the ice chest
before heading into the game
and our seats fourteen rows from third base,

where we'll watch other grown men,
called athletes and paid millions of dollars,
do what we did half an hour ago
just for fun.

Noise

I step out on my porch at 7 a.m.
the vehicular buzz already
heavy in the air.

I, listening more carefully,
hear the subtle movement of
wind through leaves
stiffening with the autumn cold.

I ponder briefly that I may never know
what a world without human noise sounds like.

I wonder briefly that some children today
may forget there's an earth outside
more interesting than what's staring,
blaring from the screen in front of them,

the artificial glow on their faces combined with the
artificial noise in their ears
creating a kind of enchanted, painless bubble
inside of which they'll float,
probably their whole lives,

and the earth will have to
lash them with hurricanes,
burn them with wildfires,
shake them with quakes,

to wake them up and remind them
the earth was here first,
and will remain here long after
it has rid itself of this noisome humanity.

Michael and I Buy Cigars on Bourbon St.

Michael and I buy cigars on Bourbon St.
and mosey down that crazy avenue in the broad daylight
with not too much sin on display
but just enough.
We gradually make our way down connecting streets
following the music of buskers, stopping here and there to listen.
A fine clarinet stops us one place,
a violin and guitar another.
We don't stop long because we have a destination.
We are heading to Pirate's Alley, to the house Faulkner lived in
        while he wrote *Soldier's Pay*,
a book neither of us has heard of before this trip.

We stop outside and finish our cigars, watching the tourists go up and down,
stick the butts in a fence to retrieve later, for we want to keep the stinking things
        as souvenirs.
We enter the store called Faulkner House Books,
spend a long time looking around, taking in the tiny rooms.
The woman who works there tells us Faulkner lived and worked in these two small rooms,
        had to borrow a washroom from neighbors.
I buy a book called *Jazz Poems*, and we head to the bar next door,
order two bourbons, sit, read some poems,
and watch a gentle rain begin.

We're in no hurry to go anywhere, the conference we're here for a far-away thought.

Every meal we've eaten seemed the best one yet,
every person we've met has made us feel welcome,
even the homeless man who yelled at us, "Hey, you dropped something."
As we turned to face him, expecting a request for money,
he said simply, smiling broadly, "You dropped your smile."
We smiled, said thanks, and moved on.

This city demands you slow down, everything cries out that in this place
you can enjoy the pleasures of life,
in fact, that's the whole point of life: to enjoy it.

And so we do, Michael and I.
We come, we slow down, we enjoy the tastes, the sounds, the smells, the joy,
until it's through, our conference done, and we head back
to that other America that tells us that Time is Money,
        that deadlines are all that matter,
        that the point of life is to work until you're too old to work,
and pleasure is just a devil's temptation.

But New Orleans has corrupted me, left its mark on my soul,
and I'll sit at my desk come Monday morning,
lean back in my chair and remember the taste of that cigar and bourbon,
      those oysters and red fish lefouche, sazerac
      and Kermit Ruffins blowing his horn, singing about his Treme woman,

and I'll know where it is I really belong.

Potroast and Poetry

Ken can't join us,
but he says, go to Aldridge's,
get the potroast.
So we do.

Harold, the proprietor, tells us
Ken's a great customer, a fine
poet. Harold has all his books.
Ken's even written
four poems for him.

He brings them out
in a green folder, pulls
a chair up to our table and
reads them to us in a fine,
Oklahoma accent.

One of them is about a
supermoon Harold saw and Ken missed.
Harold told Ken about it.
Ken went home and when he returned
he'd captured the moment for Harold in a poem.

The next one Harold reads
Ken wrote after Harold's wife died.
It's a beautiful piece. Harold almost
tears up when he reads it.
I do,
find myself looking at potroast,
okra, carrots, biscuit,
poking at my plate with my fork.

At the Lakehouse

Julie's still sleeping as I get up
and head to the kitchen,
thinking breakfast preparations,
until I see Ken on the patio
overlooking the lake
with notepad and pen
and am loathe to disturb the moment
when a poem might appear.

So I putter around until I see him stretch,
arms high above,
in what seems to betoken the moment captured.

I head out to the porch
and we talk softly so as not to wake Julie;
the remnant of last night's Romeo y Julietas
sit on the table in beds of quiet ash.

We light them up and soon are enwrapped
in thick smoke rising into the air.
Ken reads his new poem,
about mute Christians and a fiery-headed devil fool,
but that all seems far away this morning
as tobacco and flame mingle with breath
and our souls dance around us.

Listening to a Late String Quartet While Flying to Philadelphia

6:15am and the plane rises out of darkness
over a city still mostly in slumber.
The cacophony of lights below the ascending plane
spread out in a kind of chaotic order
that speaks of the humanity it hides beneath.

I am listening to Beethoven's String Quartet #14
and the opening strains are a like a prayer
that rises with the plane and me.

The technology that makes all this possible,
my flight to Philadelphia with the Quartetto Italiano,
recorded fifty years ago,
providing an exquisite soundtrack
to our rapid progress
befuddles my mind.

Because I cannot understand how any of it works,
I just accept it all with the equanimity
of an animal grazing on nature's bounty.

I cannot understand this awesome technology
any more than I can grasp how Beethoven, deaf,
composed music as beautiful as anything
ever conceived.

A frail human body hurtling 30,000 feet
above the earth
listening to a composer dead for two hundred years,
seems metaphor enough.

More Life to Lead, More Books to Read

I've more books to read than I can read.
Life is short; how short I cannot know.
I've more life to live than I can lead.

Wilt the Stilt slept with twenty thousand women;
I've got some catching up to do.
There's more life to live than I can lead.

Thomas Wolfe read twenty thousand books,
devouring whole libraries in pursuit of his art.
There are more books to read than I can read.

I joined the backpack revolution when I was young,
traveling around the world and back again,
found too much life instead, which I could not lead.

My love of books preceded my first paying job;
since then I've purchased every book I ever wanted,
long since buying more books than I can ever read.

The only thing I ever wanted was to be a poet,
experiencing life more deeply than other men.
But I discovered early to my chagrin,
there were more books to read than I could read,
there was more life to live than I could lead.

The Critic

The cat slowly approaches
my manuscript of poems

like a critic
come to pass judgment.

I wonder what it means
when he spreads the full length
of his black body

over my words,
lies there,

an expressionless look
in his mild green eyes.

Spankings, Acid, and Death

I.

I can't remember what I've done,
but I am standing in front of my father,
my pants down, his belt off.
I've been here before; I know
what stinging pain is coming.

The sound's part of it,
as the stiff leather belt descends.
The sting is excruciating;
there is in it fire's burn, and sharp electric shock.

The father's firm embrace keeps me
pinned to his knee
so I can't do the natural thing:
bolt away from such concentrated agony.

The yelp comes almost before the belt bites,
tears instantly follow—
hot, streaming, snotty, uncontrollable tears.
Sobs, body quaking sobs,
as the waspish belt strikes again and again.

My ass still stings
from ancient spankings.
My father my vision of terror,
a vision that haunts me still,
the bogeyman in my darkest dreams.

II.

On acid one time with a friend,
the door locked but not closed,
a neighbor burst in on us
crying, "It's your fairy godfather!"
the metal door careening inward
bringing an explosion of harsh daylight.
In his dark silhouette I saw black-shirted policemen
come to punish my evil ways,
but the police became my father,
with the stiff belt about to strike,

then my father became death,
and death became a spiral,
drawing me down.

III.

To this day, my image of authoritarian, fascist rule
is the police kicking down my door,
revealing themselves to be my father with a belt,
who turns out to be death come to take
all the joys of life away, insisting

somehow that it's all been my fault,
that I've done something wrong,
and I deserve what's about to happen to me.

Stone Shrine

The original shrine was just one stone
set atop another, then another,
and another.

Taking the bones of the earth
and reordering them up
and against the entropy

which constantly takes
them back down.
The building

of a primitive shrine is a declaration
to the universe that forces exist,
which can reverse course

and restack the stones,
holding them together in monuments
that mark the temporary flicker of human life.

Before I Die

I hope before I die that I meet a cellist
a very fine cellist
who loves more than anything to sit for hours
and play Bach's *Cello Suites*,
who has played *The Art of the Fugue* countless times,
loves to play Beethoven's *Late String Quartets*,
forgets to eat or sleep, this person so consumed
by the need to draw bow across strings,
fingering sounds into notes of perfection.

I want to meet this person,
want to become great friends with them,
so great that when it comes time for me to die,

they will offer to come by my bedside
play Bach and Beethoven
until my soul slips away from my body,
drifts away with the somber sounds.

If You Put the Words Together Just Right

Because if you put the words together just right, I'll weep,
tears coming down my face in uncontrollable streams,
or I'll laugh harder than I've ever laughed before,
with a different kind of tears running down my face.

If you put the words together right, you can make someone believe in God,
or you can make them turn on God forever,
or make a convincing case that whether there is or isn't a god,
it hardly matters.

If you can put the words together right,
all worlds are possible,
those real, those fantasy,
those before time and those after time's been moved beyond.

If you can put the words together right,
magic becomes real in the only place magic has ever existed:
in the imagination and the words necessary to make it live,
breathe, take on flesh and blood.

If you put the words together right,
then you understand why the Word was first,
and how the Word became flesh and lived amongst us.

Nothing to do with divinity or miracles,
everything to do with the power of words,
put in the right place,
and then all things become possible,
even resurrection,
even life after death.

Reading *The Old Man and the Sea* at Fifty

I finished reading *The Old Man and the Sea* with my students,
a book I last read over twenty years ago.
I didn't cry at the end when I read it at twenty-nine,
I didn't cry at the end when I first read it at sixteen.
But I cried this time. Perhaps because at fifty
I understand Santiago's suffering so much more viscerally,
I understand now how the body breaks down,
the knees, the shoulder, the heels of the feet.
In the book, Santiago reads about his hero, DiMaggio,
reads about heel spurs but can't understand what that means,
at least the words. He asks, "What is a spur of the heel?"
But even though the medical knowledge escapes him,
he understands deep, profound, crippling pain,
and the need to work through it anyway.
I cry at the end when Manolin finds the old man
asleep in his hut, broken by his ordeal, the boy
who has fished with Santiago since he was five,
whose parents forbid him to fish with him now
because Santiago is unlucky. I cry with Manolin,
and like him, I don't know why I cry. Something
to do with understanding how much the old man
has suffered, something to do with how much
we love this old man, who despite everything
that the sea can throw at him, endures.
Santiago said to himself while out at sea
with a half-eaten marlin, eighteen feet long,
strapped to his boat, sharks circling to take what's left,
he said, "A man can be destroyed but not defeated."
I never understood those words when I was younger.
I ask my students what they mean, and they stare at me
waiting for the answer. I tell them about Cool Hand Luke
fighting Dragline, a man a head taller than him,
a hundred pounds heavier, beating Luke to a pulp.
How Luke gets knocked down again and again,
but always, every time, he gets back up till finally
Dragline gives up, walks away, everyone walks away,
and Luke just stands there swaying, turning in circles,
moving so he won't fall down. I say, Luke was destroyed
by Dragline, but he was not defeated. He lost the fight,
but he won the love of every man who watched him
refuse to stay down. I say, Santiago refused to stay down.
He lost almost everything bringing in the skeletal remains of a marlin
bigger than anyone had ever seen, but he did not lose himself.
He will sleep, he will heal, and in a few days he will go fishing again,

this time with Manolin, who is almost a man now,
and will no longer listen to his parents who care only about luck.
He will follow this man, and he will learn how to be a great fisherman,
and he will learn how to always get up again
no matter what, until he's dead. I read this now,
at fifty, with more of my life behind me than in front,
and I know only one thing: I will always get back up again
until I can no longer rise because I am dead.

Too Late for Manly Hands

I look at the fingers holding this page,
and I realize these are the hands I'll die with.

I always wanted the hands of working men,
carpenters and cowboys, plumbers and stonemasons,
rugged, brown, covered with tiny white scars,
capable of handling tools requiring strength:
hammers, lassos, wrenches.

My father's hands, my grandfather's,
men raised on farms and ranches,
men capable of wielding mighty tools.

I watched my father hammer steel posts with a sledgehammer
deep into the earth while I held the steel beam, cowering,
as he rared back with each mighty swing
and brought the hammer down perfectly, every time,
always certain one day he'd miss and drive the hammer into my too soft head,
Abraham needlessly killing Isaac while God looked on promising nothing.

The work of reading and grading that I do now
does nothing to challenge my hands.

I think of Seamus Heaney and his pen
and know that his poem was really about shame,
shame that he was not the man his fathers were,

just a poet, weakened by the need to sit inside and read and write,
doing what has to be done.

But something in us rebels, rails angrily against the choices we have made,
demands that we head outdoors and prove our manhood
in the old ways of righteous labor.

And though we know this thinking is wrong,
that the world does not respond to or take note of its laborers,
that if we want to make a difference, it will be words, and words alone
that will get us heard,

still, it doesn't sit right somehow
and my hands stand in accusation against me.

About the Author

Hank Jones considers Texas and New Mexico, the birthplaces of his parents, to be as close to home as he knows, growing up as he did in the wake of his father's military career. After finishing a Master's in English at Tarleton State University, he taught for two years in Japan, then put a backpack on and traveled in various parts of the world until his money ran out. At that point, he got a job at his alma mater and has been teaching English there for twenty years (with a four-year stint as Assistant Director in the International Office). He received an MFA from Oklahoma City University in January 2019 and enjoyed the Oklahoma poetry scene so much, he and his wife now live in a house off Keystone Lake outside of Tulsa. His poetry has been published in *Cybersoleil: A Literary Journal*, *Voices de la Luna*, *Dragon Poet Review*, the *Concho River Review*, and *Red River Review*. He's also contributed poems to *The Great American Wise Ass Poetry Anthology* from Lamar University Literary Press, *Speak Your Mind: Poems of Protest & Resistance*, published by Village Books Press, the *Stone Renga Anthology* from Tale Feathers Press, and most recently *Bull Buffalo and Indian Paintbrush (The Poetry of Oklahoma)*, edited by Ron Wallace. What you're holding in your hands is his first book of poetry.